Who Was
Vincent van Gogh?

by Paula K. Manzanero

illustrated by Gregory Copeland

Penguin Workshop

For Gretta and Adrian—GC

PENGUIN WORKSHOP
An imprint of Penguin Random House LLC
1745 Broadway, New York, New York 10019

First published in the United States of America by Penguin Workshop,
an imprint of Penguin Random House LLC, 2025

Visit us online at penguinrandomhouse.com.

Library of Congress Cataloging-in-Publication Data is available.

Printed in the United States of America

ISBN 9780448489575 (paperback)   10 9 8 7 6 5 4 3 2 1 CJKW
ISBN 9798217140916 (library binding)   10 9 8 7 6 5 4 3 2 1 CJKW

The authorized representative in the EU for product safety and compliance
is Penguin Random House Ireland, Morrison Chambers, 32 Nassau Street,
Dublin D02 YH68, Ireland, https://eu-contact.penguin.ie.

Contents

Who Was Vincent van Gogh?

In the United States, his name is pronounced "van-GO." In England, it's "van-GOFF." The French say "van-GOG." But in his native language of Dutch, Vincent van Gogh's name is pronounced "van-GHOU-kh."

His paintings, however, are all simply signed "Vincent."

Vincent understood that his name would be difficult to pronounce in French and English. In a letter to his brother Theo, in 1888, he noted that "in future my name must be put in the catalog the way I sign it on the canvases . . . Vincent and not Van Gogh, for the excellent reason that people here wouldn't be able to pronounce that name." He was living in France at the time and had likely already heard people struggle with his last name.

Because he had worked for galleries and as an art dealer in his twenties, Vincent understood the importance of getting an artist's name "just right."

But could he have ever imagined how many galleries and art catalogs his name would appear in over time?

Probably not.

Vincent van Gogh's life was a very short one. He knew that he didn't quite fit in among the other young men of his time. He tried working at many different jobs before he finally became an artist. And he was often anxious over the details of his daily life. But he loved nature, and he found a certain peace when he was near it or surrounded by it.

Today he is one of the most famous and influential figures in the history of art. And when we see a painting signed simply "Vincent," there is no mistaking who created it.

CHAPTER 1
Early Days

Vincent Willem van Gogh was born on March 30, 1853, in a small town called Groot-Zundert in the southern part of the Netherlands. Today the town is known simply as Zundert. His father, Theodorus (called Dorus), was a minister. His mother was a very religious woman

The Netherlands

named Anna. He was the oldest of six children: Theo, Cor, Elisabeth (called Lies), Anna, and Willemina (called Wil). Vincent was named after his grandfather, who was a well-known art dealer.

Three of his uncles were also art dealers. And so the business of selling art was a large part of the Van Gogh family history.

The Dutch Reformed Church that Theodorus ministered to provided the family with a house—called a parsonage. The church also provided them a carriage, a horse, and a few servants. Groot-Zundert was a swampy rural village near the Belgian border. It was a land of wheat fields and pine forests, and it was populated by potato farmers and sheep. The parsonage had a large garden where the Van Gogh children each had their own plot of land to plant.

The family was very close. After church on Sundays they would gather around the piano and sing. Every day, they walked together for an hour. And every night, they read aloud to one another. Their favorite books were by Charles Dickens and Hans Christian Andersen. Young Vincent thought Andersen's fairy tales were "glorious . . . so beautiful and real."

Vincent's mother encouraged him to draw when he was very young. In fact, all the Van Gogh children learned to draw from Anna, who gave them her own drawings to trace and color. Vincent was very close to his mother.

Hans Christian Andersen (1805–1875)

Hans Christian Andersen was born in Odense, Denmark. He wrote plays, novels, and poems. But he is most famous for his beloved fairy tales, which he began publishing in 1835. These include "The Ugly Duckling," "The Emperor's New Clothes," "The Red Shoes," and "The Princess and the Pea."

One of his best-known fairy tales is "The Little Mermaid," the story of a mermaid who falls in love with a human prince. She gives up her life in the sea for the possibility to live on land and remain with her prince. Although written in 1837, the story has been animated for film many times in many languages throughout the twentieth century. And a live-action film version was released in 2023.

He was also very close to his brother Theo. The boys shared an attic bedroom, where they would often stay up late, talking and reading novels like *The Swiss Family Robinson*. Theo, who had been born just after Vincent turned four, adored his big brother. In the summer, the boys hiked in the fields around Groot-Zundert. In the winter, they went sledding and ice-skating. Vincent taught Theo how to build sandcastles and play board games. Although they shared many of the same interests, the boys were quite different. Blond-haired Theo was friendly and outgoing, while Vincent—whose hair was bright red—was more distant and shy. Vincent took long walks alone and collected wildflowers, birds' nests, and beetles.

The young Van Gogh children were taught at home by their mother and a governess. A governess is a woman who works as a private teacher for the children of one household.

In 1860, when Vincent was seven, he attended the village school. Even though he could read very well, he did not do well in his classes. In 1864, when he was eleven, Vincent was sent away to a boarding school in Zevenbergen, which was about sixteen miles from his home. He was the youngest student there, and he felt very out of place. Two years later, young Vincent asked to return home. However, his parents decided to send him even farther away, to a new middle school in Tilburg, instead. It was a fancy public school in a former royal palace. There he studied Dutch, German, English, French, history, zoology, gymnastics,

and art. In art class, he learned to "sketch the impression the object makes rather than the object itself." But even art lessons couldn't make up for his loneliness. While all the other boys at school lived at home with their loved ones, Vincent had to board with a local family.

The Tilburg school

In 1868, just weeks before he turned fifteen and a few months before the end of the school year, Vincent walked out of the Tilburg school. He had had enough of his formal education. Carrying his bags, he made his way home to Groot-Zundert. His parents did not approve, but Vincent was just happy to be back.

CHAPTER 2
Becoming an Artist

Vincent's uncle Cent helped him to find a job with an art dealer in a city about an hour north of Groot-Zundert: The Hague, which is the center of government for the Netherlands.

The Hague

This was a lucky break! Vincent got to look at art every day at work. Even on his days off, he would visit the museums of nearby Amsterdam, where he could study the Dutch masters, the greatest artists of the Dutch golden age.

Vincent's boss at the art gallery thought the young man was responsible and hardworking. In August 1872, fifteen-year-old Theo spent a few days visiting Vincent in The Hague. By the

end of that year, Theo decided to leave school, just as Vincent had earlier. With the help of his uncle Cent, he, too, found a job with an art dealer. But Theo would be working in Belgium, far away from The Hague.

The Netherlands

The brothers wrote to each other often—at least a few times each month—about art, life, and family.

Vincent worked to complete his training and was eventually given a promotion. But his new position was at the company's London office, and he would be even farther away from Theo. Vincent moved to London in 1873.

The Dutch Masters

The golden age of Dutch painting refers roughly to the work made in the 1600s.

During this time, the Dutch Republic was the most prosperous nation in Europe. Scientific developments and global trade had reshaped people's understanding of their own place in the world. Artists were influenced by these historical and religious changes. And Dutch artists began to break with long-standing Catholic traditions. Instead of creating religious paintings of scenes from the Bible, they began to paint real-life subjects, including portraits, landscapes, still lifes, seascapes, and ships.

The most famous painters from this period—known as the Dutch masters—are Rembrandt van Rijn, Frans Hals, and Johannes Vermeer. Vermeer's *Girl with a Pearl Earring* is one of the most famous

Girl with a Pearl Earring

paintings in the world, and it was created during this artistic era.

One of the few female artists to be included as one of the Dutch old masters was Rachel Ruysch. The daughter of a botanist, she enjoyed a successful career as a still life painter whose main subject was stunningly detailed floral arrangements.

And he was very happy there. He wrote to Theo about the museums, gardens, and galleries in London. At age twenty, Vincent was successful and was earning even more than his father. He celebrated his promotion and his move to England by buying a new top hat and gloves.

London was a bustling city, and Vincent was delighted by the energy of it. He lived in a boardinghouse (a house where guests pay for

a single room and their meals) and finally had a room "without a slanting ceiling."

Vincent soon became interested in dating his landlady's daughter Eugenie, who was already engaged to another man. He proposed to Eugenie more than once, even though she was already in a relationship with someone else. Becoming a couple was out of the question. In 1875, he was transferred to the Paris gallery of the art dealer he worked for. Vincent was not happy about it. Still, Uncle Cent thought that the change would be good for his shy twenty-two-year-old nephew.

Uncle Cent

Vincent appreciated the Louvre Museum, the Parisian galleries, and the Luxembourg Palace.

Luxembourg Palace

But his job in Paris didn't last long. Vincent worked there for only two months, and he was sad and lonely. He missed his family. He wrote many letters to Theo, adding doodles to them, describing his life in Paris.

During Christmas 1876, Vincent returned to the Netherlands to visit his family, who had moved to the town of Etten. At this time, he became much more serious about his faith and his religion. He even considered becoming a Dutch Reformed pastor, like his father.

Van Gogh's 1876 drawing of Etten

But he returned to Paris, where he was promptly fired from his job for being rude to the customers. Vincent then moved back to London. He found a job teaching at a small run-down boarding school there. He received no salary, only food and a room to stay in. When his job as a teacher didn't work out, Vincent once again thought seriously about religious careers, like becoming a missionary or a minister.

The Louvre

The Louvre Museum was established in 1793 in the medieval-era Louvre Palace in Paris, France. It contains about 35,000 objects, including paintings, sculptures, drawings, and archaeological objects from thousands of years ago up to the twenty-first century.

The enormous collection of the Louvre is divided among eight departments, including Paintings, Sculptures, Prints and Drawings, and others. A few

of its most famous works of art are the statues of the Venus de Milo and the Winged Victory of Samothrace. The most famous painting in its collection is the *Mona Lisa*, by Leonardo da Vinci.

In 1984, Chinese American architect I. M. Pei designed the now-famous glass pyramid entrance to the museum in its Napoleon courtyard.

The Louvre is the largest—and the most-visited—museum in the world. Nearly nine million people visited the museum in 2023 alone.

He failed the University of Amsterdam entrance examination in 1878 and then failed a course at a Protestant missionary school as well. But that didn't stop Vincent from getting assigned a missionary job in Belgium.

To show his support of the poor people living in the coal-mining district, he gave his comfortable room to a homeless person and moved into a small shed, where he slept on a pile of straw on the floor. Some families in the community appreciated Vincent's efforts. They needed all the help and support they could get. But others thought he was strange. To make fun of him, children threw things at him when he passed them on the street.

One of the greatest difficulties Vincent had with his assignment in Brussels was that he was shy. He wasn't comfortable speaking to groups of people, which is very important to the job of being a preacher. The church decided that he wasn't dignified enough to become a pastor, and Vincent was dismissed. Now without a direction for his life, Vincent began walking on a long journey that would eventually lead him back to his parents' home in Etten.

In total, he walked eighty-five miles, sleeping in hay and trading drawings for food.

He had tried to be a teacher, an art dealer, a bookseller, and a preacher. And he had not succeeded at any of these jobs. When his brother Theo suggested that he study art, Vincent decided to get serious about learning anatomy (the study of the human body) and perspective (the representation of three-dimensional objects in art) to create better artwork. In November 1880, he returned to Brussels to attend the Royal Academy of Fine Arts. He spent six months studying the Dutch masters and drawing models.

By the spring of the following year, he was back home in Etten, where he continued to draw and paint, using different materials like charcoal, pastels, and watercolors.

Anton Mauve

In 1881, Vincent's cousin Anton agreed to have him as a student in The Hague. Anton Mauve, who was a successful artist, introduced Vincent to oil paint and how to really "capture" what he saw. Up to this point, Vincent had mostly spent his time drawing. Anton even lent him money to set up a studio, where Vincent first began seriously painting in oils. He borrowed money from Theo to buy oil paint, which he spread thickly on his canvases and then worked over with his paintbrush. He was pleased with the results.

Many of Vincent's letters to Theo at this time were about money. His lack of it was a very real concern. Vincent felt certain that if he moved to the country, his studio wouldn't cost quite so much and even food would be cheaper. "Oh, Theo, I could make much more progress if I was a little better off," he wrote.

In September 1883, he left The Hague and eventually returned to his parents' home. By this time, they were living in the town of Nuenen. Vincent began to focus on drawing and painting, now working mostly outside. He learned to sketch and paint quickly, creating images of the weavers—the men who worked on looms to create cotton and linen cloth—and their cottages in the area.

In May, he painted *The Parsonage Garden at Nuenen*. Perhaps it reminded him of the parsonage and garden of his childhood back in Groot-Zundert.

Dorus and Anna's home in Nuenen

He stayed in Nuenen for two years, living in a space he had rented from a local Catholic church. He painted in a small, dark bedroom he used as his studio and slept in a space in the attic. During his time in Nuenen, he completed nearly two hundred oil paintings. But they were not created with the bright colors we see today when we look at Vincent's artwork. These were much more serious and were mostly done in dark brown tones. Because the great Dutch masters had used earthy-brown, dark green, and tan colors to create their paintings, Vincent did, too.

Vincent was in the habit of sending his drawings to Theo, who was still working as an art dealer. Theo had always been supportive. He planned to eventually show Vincent's paintings to collectors and to other art dealers in Paris. In May 1885, Vincent sent his brother *The Potato Eaters*. This was Vincent's first major oil painting, and some say his first masterpiece. Vincent was thirty-two when he painted it.

The Potato Eaters

The Potato Eaters shows the De Groot family around their dinner table, eating potatoes and drinking coffee. Vincent wanted to show the farmers of Nuenen as they really were, in a natural and unfussy setting. Theo noted that Vincent's work was very dark and not much like the impressionist paintings that were being sold in Paris at the time.

Impressionism

The art movement known as impressionism began in Paris during the 1870s and 1880s. The painting style of impressionism is characterized by small, visible brushstrokes that can sometimes show just the impression of a form (rather than a realistic depiction of it), unblended colors, and—perhaps most importantly—the accurate representation of natural light.

Impressionist painters often painted outdoors in the sunlight. They wanted to capture the changing qualities of light and the beauty of wide-open natural scenes on their canvases. This was considered radical at the time.

Some of the most famous impressionist painters are Pierre-Auguste Renoir, Claude Monet, Mary Cassatt, Édouard Manet, Edgar Degas, and Berthe Morisot.

Two of the most famous impressionist paintings were painted by Monet: *Impression, Sunrise* (1872) and *Bridge over a Pond of Water Lilies* (1899).

Bridge over a Pond of Water Lilies

CHAPTER 3
Vincent and Theo in Paris

Belgium

In 1885, Vincent moved to Antwerp in Belgium. He stayed in a room above a paint seller. Theo sent him money so that he could eat and pay his rent. But Vincent spent the money on paint supplies, coffee, and tobacco instead of food. Although his health suffered, he managed to study color more closely and learned how to mix it properly in his paints. He still had not sold a painting. Vincent was determined to incorporate some of the brightness he had seen in impressionist art. He began to use more red, green, purple, and blue. He visited museums and studied the paintings of great artists like Peter Paul Rubens.

Vincent took—and passed—the entrance exams to study at the Royal Academy of Fine Arts in Antwerp. In January 1886, he began painting and drawing there. But he fought with his teachers over painting styles and techniques. When Vincent was asked to draw the classical Greek sculpture of a goddess titled Venus de Milo, he drew a poor peasant woman instead. When his professor corrected the drawing, Vincent became angry and shouted at him. And this may have been the last class he attended at the Academy of Fine Arts.

The Royal Academy of Fine Arts, Antwerp

His time there was very short-lived. By March of
that same year, he had moved to Paris.

Vincent moved in with Theo and began

painting portraits, still life paintings, and street scenes of Parisian neighborhoods. He wrote to a friend: "There is but one Paris, and however hard living may be here . . . the French air clears up the brain and does one . . . a world of good." He painted outdoor scenes including *View of Paris* and *The 14th of July, 1886*, which shows the joyful celebration of the French National Day.

View of Paris

Peter Paul Rubens (1577–1640)

Peter Paul Rubens was a seventeenth-century Flemish artist and diplomat from Antwerp who became one of the most influential artists of the golden age of Dutch art. As a young man, he traveled to Italy and Spain to study classical and Renaissance art.

Rubens blended realism (an art style with accurate, realistic, and detailed images of life) with the styles of the Italian Renaissance to create paintings that came to be called "baroque." The baroque style of art is known for showing dramatic lighting, deep colors, and powerful human figures in motion in paintings of historical, religious, and mythological themes.

Rubens painted portraits, landscapes, and historical paintings as well as altarpieces (paintings on wood that are displayed behind an altar). Rubens is especially known for his paintings of women with particularly soft, full-figured bodies and rosy skin tones. It is from his name that the term "Rubenesque" is derived, meaning to have a full and shapely body.

After the paintings of several impressionists became more well-known, other artists, including Vincent, began using new techniques and even bolder colors. They wanted to portray more emotion in their work. They didn't always use the most natural or "correct" colors for their subjects. These artists would come to be known as the postimpressionists.

At this time, new ideas in art seemed to be springing up all over Paris. Vincent met the artists Edgar Degas, Claude Monet, and Henri de Toulouse-Lautrec, who painted a portrait of him.

Edgar Degas   Claude Monet

He met Georges Seurat, who was a master of pointillist painting—a new and revolutionary style of painting where tiny dots applied to the canvas create a larger image and blend of colors when seen from a distance. In 1886, two

Henri de Toulouse-Lautrec

large exhibitions in Paris showcased pointillism in paintings for the first time, displaying the work of Georges Seurat and Paul Signac.

The impressionist paintings had inspired Vincent to move on from the dreary earth tones of his early work. He began to use very bright colors and to show fewer dark shadows in his own paintings. And he began to use bigger brushstrokes. In Paris, he also became interested in Japanese woodcuts called ukiyo-e. Vincent used the hundreds of ukiyo-e woodblocks he had collected to decorate his studio. And he eventually used some elements of this Japanese style in his own paintings.

In his *Portrait of Père Tanguy* of 1887, the Japanese prints that Vincent loved are shown on the wall in the background of Julien Tanguy's portrait. There is even a print of Mount Fuji painted just above Julien's head. Julien was a man who sold art supplies in Paris. *Père* is French for "father."

Portrait of Père Tanguy

And some artists in Paris called Julien that because he was so kind and generous to them. The influences of the other painters Vincent knew in Paris at this time are easy to spot in this painting as well, especially in the bright colors and visible brushstrokes.

Theo encouraged Vincent. He always told him how good his paintings were, so alive and filled with movement. But Vincent was not easy to get along with at all times. In early 1887, Vincent began to spend much of his time away from Paris, in a suburb called Asnières, where he would draw and paint. He befriended the pointillist painter Georges Seurat. Vincent began using some elements of pointillism, including the use of complementary colors— those with opposite hues.

Georges Seurat

Ukiyo-e

The Great Wave

The Japanese art form known as ukiyo-e originated in the city of Edo (present-day Tokyo) in 1615 and continued for more than 250 years. Wooden blocks were carved and then covered in paint. The blocks were then pressed onto paper to make the woodblock prints. The carvings often depicted the everyday life and surroundings of people living in Japan at the time.

The most famous ukiyo-e woodblock print is called *Under the Wave off Kanagawa*. It shows a large cresting wave in a stormy sea near Mount Fuji. Also called *The Great Wave*, it was created by the artist Hokusai in 1831.

The vibrant contrasts of blue and orange, and yellow and purple, would become a recognizable feature of Vincent's paintings. Some people believe these contrasting colors were also a symbol of his inner struggles. Although he wanted to be near Theo and to work with other artists, Vincent was headstrong and often worked best when alone.

In Asnières, he painted outdoor scenes of parks, restaurants, and the Seine River. In the summer, he painted *Self-Portrait with Straw Hat*

Self-Portrait with Straw Hat

in oil paint on cardboard. At the end of the year, Vincent exhibited his art in a show that was noted as ahead of anything happening at that time in Paris. Theo and Vincent became friends with the artist Paul Gauguin, a self-taught painter, sculptor, and printmaker, who used woodblock and wood-engraving techniques. During the 1880s, he showed his work with the impressionists in Paris. Vincent exchanged

Paul Gauguin

some of his paintings with those of Gauguin, who was clearly one of the most important painters at the time.

The cold winters and the pace of life in and around Paris grew tiring to Vincent. He longed for a slower pace and a quieter place to work.

In early 1888, he moved to Arles, a village in the Provence region of Southern France. Although less than five hundred miles away from Paris, it was almost another world.

CHAPTER 4
Arles

The countryside, farms, and fields of Arles all delighted Vincent. The sunlight was brighter there. He was inspired to use more yellow in his paintings, and much brighter blues. He wanted to capture all the local scenes: wheat fields and rural scenes of harvesting. By this time, Vincent had a bad smoker's cough. Maybe the fresh air would be good for his health—it certainly seemed to cheer him up.

In May 1888, Vincent moved into rooms at the Café de la Gare in Arles. Later that year, he painted *Café Terrace at Night*. The dark night of the painting is brightened by the gas lamps shining through the café windows and the stars in the sky. But Vincent wanted a proper studio and a gallery where he could display his work. He rented part of a building called the Yellow House to use as his studio. Downstairs there were two rooms: a studio and a kitchen. Upstairs were two bedrooms. By September, Vincent had moved from the café to the Yellow House. His landlords were Joseph and Marie Ginoux.

The Yellow House

Once he was set up at the Yellow House, Vincent painted all the time. He painted pictures of his room, his furniture, and the Yellow House itself. He even painted his muddy shoes in a number of still lifes. *Shoes*, from 1888, is a simple painting of a pair of worn shoes sitting on the tile floor of his room. In one span of just twenty-six days, Vincent painted eighteen paintings!

He visited the town of Saintes-Maries to paint images of the village and boats on the sea. *Seascape near Les Saintes-Maries-de-la-Mer* shows three boats on a calm sea and many shades of blue in the sea and sky. The painting reveals how expressive Vincent's style was becoming at this time. He used impasto—a term that means laying the paint on thickly—to create the waves. He did this by squeezing the tubes of paint directly onto his canvas. With so much paint on the surface of his work, he could then create texture with a palette knife rather than a paintbrush.

(A palette knife is an artist's tool usually used for mixing and applying paints.)

Some of Vincent's paintings took weeks to dry because of how thick the paint was. Even now, Vincent's paintings are almost instantly recognizable by the chunky impasto applied to his canvases. He often used these lumpy strokes of thick paint to convey the magical quality of the bright sun and the stunning beauty of the natural world.

Vincent was working very hard, but he still hadn't earned any money as a painter. He bought paint, brushes, and canvas with the allowance that Theo sent him. When he couldn't afford canvas, he painted on cardboard or burlap. He painted himself, in quite a few self-portraits, when he couldn't afford to pay models. Theo begged him to slow down, to use less paint. He knew that collectors wanted carefully finished artwork, not furiously paint-splashed paintings.

"I have sometimes worked excessively fast. . . .
I can't help it," Vincent said. He was driven to
create more and more pieces, and it showed in
his work.

Van Gogh's painting on burlap

Theo was not wealthy. But he wanted to
support Vincent both financially and emotionally
so that he could paint as much as he wanted to.
Theo believed in his brother and never turned
down a request for money.

Theo van Gogh

Vincent painted all day in the hot sun. Legend has it, at night he painted with candles stuck into his hat so that he could see his canvas! The people in Arles thought he was very strange. He had no friends. He sold no paintings. But he was creating! Vincent's paintings from this time all show bold colors, dramatic and expressive brushwork, and a passionate, daring artistic style.

He wrote many letters to his friend Paul Gauguin, finally convincing him to visit Arles. Vincent got busy painting four versions of sunflowers in one week to decorate the studio before Gauguin's arrival. He wrote to Theo: "I'd like to do a decoration for the studio. Nothing but large sunflowers." He bought two beds for the Yellow House and had a table and chairs made. Vincent was in a hurry to furnish the rooms in time for his friend's arrival. He sometimes created two sunflower paintings in a single  day. In addition to the many sunflower paintings, he painted *Gauguin's Chair* with a candle and two books on the seat, and *Van Gogh's Chair* with his own pipe and a pouch of tobacco.

Fingerprints in the Impasto

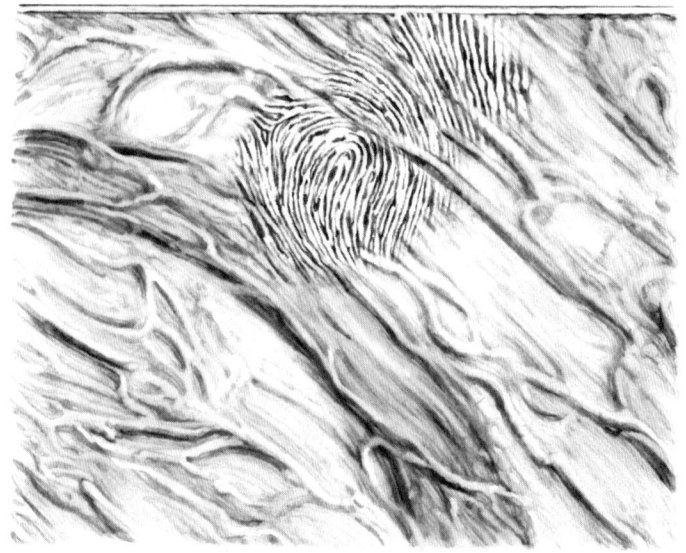

In 2024, a large fingerprint was found by a curator on a small painting at the national museum in Amsterdam. *View of Amsterdam from Central Station*, by Vincent van Gogh, was painted in October 1885. Vincent would have painted this view of the city at Central Station, then most likely hurriedly carried it to the museum, where he was meeting a friend—permanently setting his thumbprint in the thick impasto.

Because he painted quickly, used hefty globs of paint, and often painted outside (carrying his canvases while still wet), fingerprints can be seen in a few of Vincent's paintings, including *Summer Evening* (1888) and *The Olive Trees* (1889). There are even traces of insects in a couple of his paintings. *The Olive Trees* has both a fingerprint and the remains of a grasshopper!

Vincent was painting very quickly now. The collection of thirty paintings he created in preparation for Gauguin's arrival at the Yellow House is now known as the *Decoration of the Yellow House*. It begins with the four sunflower paintings, followed by four portraits (including that of the town's postal supervisor Joseph Roulin in *Portrait of Joseph Roulin*), and then more than twenty paintings between August and the end of 1888.

Portrait of Joseph Roulin

Vincent had been hoping to convince his friend to help him establish an artist's colony, or "collective" for painters to work together. In October 1888, Gauguin finally arrived in Arles. Together the men visited the city of Montpellier, near the Mediterranean Sea, farther south of Arles. They visited the Musée Fabre and closely studied paintings by famous artists such as Gustave Courbet. Vincent painted a portrait of Gauguin that he called *Man in a Red Beret*.

Vincent was happy to have Gauguin with him, as a friend and as an equal. Two painters, working together. But Vincent was stubborn. And Paul Gauguin could be aggressive and pushy. He considered himself to be the superior artist. The two men fought constantly. Vincent feared that Gauguin would soon leave his just-forming artist colony in Arles.

Musée Fabre

CHAPTER 5
Self-Portrait with Bandaged Ear

After a few days of heavy rain, during which both men were stuck inside the Yellow House, tensions grew. Vincent and Gauguin argued about artistic inspiration and each other's methods. Vincent thought that it was best to work from nature (by standing in a field or studying a vase of flowers) while Gauguin believed in working from his own imagination and memory. Gauguin may have even made the decision to move out and into a nearby hotel. But it's not certain. What we do know is that on the night of December 23, Vincent became so distraught by the arguing that he used a straight razor to cut off most of his own ear, leaving just the bottom lobe. He bandaged his wound as best he could. He then wrapped his severed ear in newspaper and delivered it to a young woman named Gabrielle, who worked nearby.

Vincent was found by a police officer and taken to the hospital. He was treated by a young

doctor named Felix Rey. Too much time had passed for Dr. Rey to be able to reattach the ear. Vincent said he had no memory of cutting his ear. Could he have blacked out? Could he have had a complete mental breakdown? Vincent stayed in the hospital.

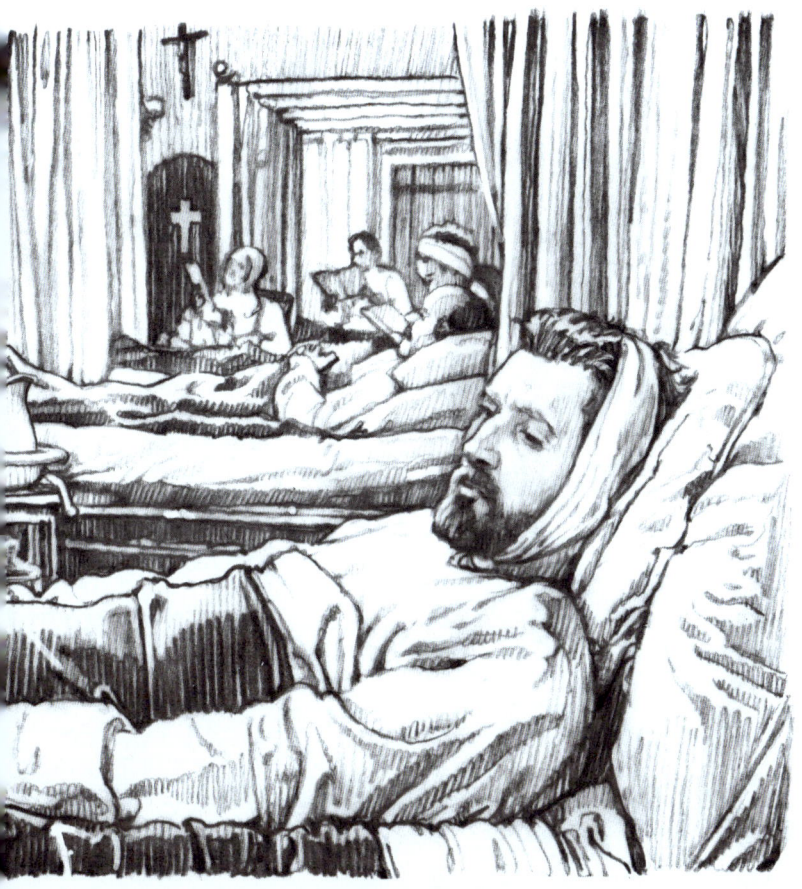

Johanna Bonger

Paul Gauguin let Theo know what had happened. The very next night, Theo took a train to Arles, arriving on Christmas Day to see Vincent. But he returned to Paris that night. He had just become engaged to Johanna Bonger and wanted to spend part of the holiday with her.

Although Vincent repeatedly asked for Gauguin while he was in the hospital, the painter had quickly left for Paris. Gauguin never visited Vincent in the hospital or saw him again. Joseph Roulin, the postmaster, did visit with Vincent.

In the new year, Vincent returned to the Yellow House. He painted himself in *Self-Portrait with Bandaged Ear.* But he was not well. He began hallucinating (experiencing sights and sounds that are not real) and spent much of his time back at the hospital. The people of Arles began describing him as "the redheaded madman" and created a petition, asking the police to close up his house. In March, Vincent returned to stay in the hospital.

In April, floods badly damaged paintings stored at the Yellow House. Vincent moved into rooms that were owned by Dr. Rey. While

Dr. Felix Rey

there, he painted the *Portrait of Doctor Felix Rey* as a gift to the doctor before leaving to stay in an asylum (a hospital that offers support for those who are mentally ill) in the town of Saint-Rémy, less than twenty miles from Arles.

The asylum that Vincent arrived at in May 1889, Saint-Paul-de-Mausole, had once been a monastery. He had two rooms in the clinic, one for his room, the other to use as a studio. "I have never been so peaceful as here and in the hospital at Arles—to be able to paint a little at last," he wrote.

Saint-Paul-de-Mausole

In July, he received a letter from Theo's wife, Johanna, with "a great piece of news" that they were expecting a baby. Vincent replied that he was very glad to hear it. The good news cheered Vincent up and seemed to restore his confidence.

Vincent began to re-create the interior of the hospital and the gardens there in paintings such as *Vestibule in the Asylum* and drawings like *Garden of the Hospital*. He painted several different images of the irises that grew in the hospital garden. These paintings show strong outlines around the flowers and leaves, as well as more influences of the Japanese woodblock prints Vincent liked so much. He took supervised walks and painted cypress trees, olive trees, and the countryside. In June of that year, he painted *The Starry Night*, his most well-known painting, and one of the most recognizable paintings in the world.

The Starry Night was inspired by the view from Vincent's room, just before sunrise. In it, he painted huge stars glowing with the silvery texture of thickly applied paint. Spirals seem to swoop and swirl over the mountaintops, while two cypress trees tower over the left side of the painting. The moon burns brightly in the sky.

The Starry Night

This was the way Vincent saw the night sky: reimagined through the scenes of his past. It is a sky that is not typical or ordinary in any way. It shows limitless possibilities and endless wonder.

Theo thought the brushwork and color of Vincent's work at this time was becoming "very curious." It was true—Vincent's style was unusual then. But Theo wrote to his brother that "in the course of time [Vincent's paintings] will become very beautiful . . . and they will undoubtedly be appreciated someday."

Portrait of Doctor Felix Rey

The painting *Portrait of Doctor Felix Rey* shows Dr. Rey with a beard and mustache, wearing a blue coat. The background is a sea of green with bright yellow swirls. When Dr. Rey received the gift of his portrait from Vincent, he didn't like the painting very much at all. He used it to repair his chicken coop, and then, in 1901, he sold it.

It is now on display in the Pushkin Museum of Fine Arts in Moscow and is valued at more than $50 million.

In addition to the outdoor scenes that he was limited to by the grounds of the asylum, he painted some interpretations (new versions) of other artists' paintings, like Jean-François Millet's *The Sower*. His illness very much affected his work. He asked Theo and his mother to send him some of his earlier drawings so that he could use them as inspiration for new paintings. He also mentioned that the food at the asylum tasted moldy. He wasn't used to the steady diet of chickpeas, beans, and lentils.

When Theo and Johanna's son was born on January 31, 1890, Vincent "started right away to make a picture for him, to hang in their bedroom, branches of white almond blossom against a blue sky." The baby was named Vincent Willem after his uncle. The painting is called *Almond Blossom*.

CHAPTER 6
Seventy Paintings in Seventy Days

The year 1890 began on a positive note for Vincent. In January, he was described as a "genius" in a review of an exhibit that appeared in a French literary magazine. The reviewer hailed his "brilliant and dazzling symphonies of color and lines." He also noted that Vincent had a passion for, and an obsession with, sunflowers. And then, something wonderful happened. Out of the six paintings that Vincent had exhibited, one actually sold. This was the first painting that Vincent sold from an exhibition.

In February, Vincent painted four portraits of Madame Ginoux, based on a sketch Gauguin had made of her over a year earlier. He seemed to be painting nonstop.

In the spring, ten of his paintings, including *The Starry Night* and *Irises*, were included in an exhibit of the Société des Artistes Indépendants (Society of Independent Artists) in Paris.

The Red Vineyard

The Red Vineyards at Arles, known simply as *The Red Vineyard*, is an oil painting by Vincent van Gogh that was made on burlap in early November 1888. It is painted in bright yellow, orange, blue, purple, and green.

In 1890, the painting was bought by Anna Boch, a Belgian painter and collector and the sister of the impressionist painter Eugène Boch. At the time, Anna paid four hundred francs (which would be about $2,250 today) for the painting, making this the only painting of Van Gogh's that was sold during his lifetime.

Theo wrote to Vincent, "I've received the money for your painting from Brussels. . . . I'm holding it for whenever you want it."

In 1909, Anna Boch sold *The Red Vineyard*, and it was eventually moved to the Pushkin Museum of Fine Arts in Moscow, where it remains today.

The society had been founded in 1884, and its annual shows often set the trends of new art styles. That meant more and more people were becoming aware of Vincent's art, and more collectors were asking Theo about it. Theo praised Vincent's latest paintings, saying they had an "unshakable something which nature has, even in her fiercest aspects." Claude Monet said Vincent's work was the best in the show.

In May 1890, Vincent left the asylum and moved to the suburbs of Paris. He was now living in Auvers, less than thirty miles from the city center. He wanted to be closer to Theo, Johanna, and their new baby.

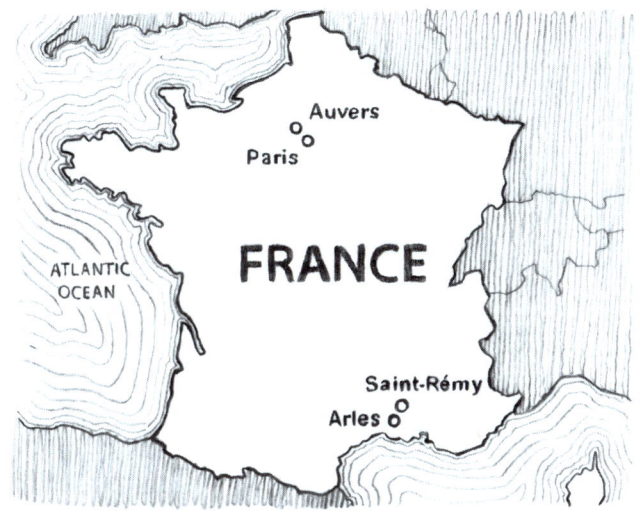

Vincent seemed to be painting all the time. He began nearly eighty paintings, completing seventy of them in just seventy days—some of which became his most famous works. He had become completely captivated by the countryside of Auvers, which he described as "very beautiful, having among other things a lot of old thatched roofs." Vincent loved the green hills, the blue of the sky, and all the delicate yellow of the wheat fields. He painted *Thatched Cottages*, *The Church at Auvers*, and *Marguerite Gachet at the Piano*.

The Church at Auvers

In Auvers, Vincent had met Dr. Paul Gachet, who treated patients with nervous disorders. Dr. Gachet invited Vincent to dinner and offered to look after him if he was feeling sick or anxious. The two men discussed art and literature. Vincent eventually painted a portrait of Dr. Gachet, in which he looks tired and sad. It seems to reflect what Vincent had written to Theo about the doctor: "I think he is sicker than I am."

Dr. Paul Gachet

In June, Theo and Johanna brought their new baby to Auvers for a visit. The brothers were so happy to see each other, they hugged and cried. Vincent proudly carried his nephew to Dr. Gachet's home to show him the cats, dogs, chickens, and rabbits that lived there. The family had a picnic and took a long walk together. It was a happy, peaceful day. Vincent was content to be living closer to Theo and his family now.

But he was also lonely. And his sadness could be extreme. He recognized that some of the beauty around him was clouded by "turbulent skies."

His ear had been badly damaged, and the wound was painful. He drank too much alcohol. He argued with the townspeople who mocked him.

In July, he painted *Wheat Field with Crows* and *Tree Roots*, two of the last paintings he would ever complete. Less than ten years earlier, Vincent had written to Theo that his watercolors of tree roots expressed something of life's struggles. *Wheat Field with Crows* is a dark and serious painting. It is very different from the bright skies and sunny scenes Vincent had been painting for the past few years. Was Vincent losing hope?

Wheat Field with Crows

On the morning of July 27, 1890, Vincent was painting in a wheat field near a local barn. For reasons we may never understand, he shot himself in the chest. Whether on purpose or accidentally, we do not know. Where the gun came from, and why he had it, is also a mystery. What we do know is that, by that evening, he had managed to walk back to the inn in Auvers. He was treated by two doctors, one of whom was Dr. Gachet, and the innkeeper Arthur Ravoux. By the time Theo arrived the next day, Vincent was suffering from an infection of the wound near his heart. He died on July 29. He was only thirty-seven years old.

Vincent was buried the very next day in Auvers, in a little cemetery behind a church he had once painted. His coffin was covered in white linen and strewn with yellow sunflowers and dahlias. His brushes and easel were placed in front of it. His brother Theo died less than a year later, in January 1891, and he was buried in the city of Utrecht in the Netherlands. More than twenty years later, Theo's widow, Johanna, had his body moved to Auvers to be reburied next to his brother Vincent.

CHAPTER 7
The End, but Also a Beginning

Although Vincent had placed an order for more paint only a few days earlier, which people took as a hopeful sign of determination to keep working, he died with a heartbreaking unfinished letter to Theo in his pocket. It read in part: "Well, I risk my life for my own work . . . but what can you do—"

We are still unsure what medical diagnosis Vincent might have been given if he were alive today. His periods of anxiety or depression seem to have been made worse by his constant work schedule, a poor diet, lack of sleep, stress, and heavy alcohol consumption.

Over the course of the two brothers' lives, Vincent had written Theo almost one thousand letters! Luckily for future generations, Theo kept every single one. (Yet Vincent, always the more awkward, older brother, kept only a select few.)

Through these letters, we can learn much of what Vincent felt and thought throughout his short life. They are a testament to Theo's love for his older brother—even to this day.

Although he was a mystery to his neighbors—and often mocked by the people of Auvers—after his death, Vincent's paintings began gaining attention from critics and art dealers. In fact, he has become the very symbol of a misunderstood genius—someone who was not fully appreciated

during their lifetime but who has been celebrated after their death.

Theo remained alive just long enough to hold a memorial exhibition of Vincent's work. But after his death, it was up to Johanna to keep Vincent's paintings available for people to see. Within ten years, she had organized exhibitions of his work and found interested collectors. Vincent's paintings were now selling in Europe and the United States.

The Van Gogh Museum in Amsterdam, which opened in 1973, is an archive of Vincent's drawings, letters, and objects from his daily life. Vincent's nephew wanted to be sure that anyone interested in Vincent's art and legacy had the chance to view all that he had inherited from his parents, Theo and Johanna. Vincent's paintings are also on view in the most famous museums in the world, including the Museum of Modern Art in New York, the Musée d'Orsay in Paris, and the National Gallery in London.

The Van Gogh Museum

In 1990, exactly one hundred years after it had been painted, *Portrait of Dr. Gachet* was sold at auction for $82.5 million. At that time, it was the world's most expensive painting. Vincent had described it as "sad but gentle, yet clear and intelligent, that is how many portraits ought to be done. . . . There are modern heads [portraits] that may perhaps be looked at for a long time, and that may perhaps be looked back on with longing a hundred years later." And he was right.

Self-Portrait with Grey Felt Hat

One of those "heads" was Vincent's own. Over his lifetime, he painted thirty-six self-portraits. They are instantly recognizable by Vincent's red hair, beard, slim features, and intense stare. One of them, *Self-Portrait with Grey Felt Hat*, was painted in Paris in 1887. But it was reimagined for a new generation in 2023—as a Pokémon card!

Although he sold only one exhibited painting during his lifetime, Vincent is among the most famous and influential painters in the world today. And even though he worked seriously as an artist for only ten years, he created more than two thousand artworks, including more than 850 oil paintings. It's amazing to consider that most of these were completed in the last two years of his life!

Pikachu with Grey Felt Hat

The Van Gogh Museum in Amsterdam partnered with the Japanese company Pokémon in 2023 for a very special event. For the exhibit, Pokémon created a limited-edition themed collection of cards and products. On the opening day of the show, the museum was swarmed with visitors trying to buy handfuls of items that depicted the Pikachu character looking very much like Vincent van Gogh. The commemorative special foil card *Pikachu with Grey Felt Hat*, designed by Naoyo Kimura, matches

the style of Vincent's bold pointillist portrait. It sold out within hours.

Visitors to the Van Gogh Museum today are limited to purchasing just one highly collectible card per person.

Vincent's unique style inspired many artists throughout the twentieth century, including Pablo Picasso, who named Vincent as one of his main inspirations. The vitality of his work—the quality that makes it seem to come alive—makes it popular around the world even today, where you can see paintings like *The Starry Night* reproduced on posters, sweatshirts, phone cases, sneakers, and night-lights. You can even step into a Van Gogh painting in "immersive" exhibits that project moving images of Vincent's paintings on

huge gallery walls to make you feel as if you are back at Arles or Auvers with him.

His choice of vivid colors, his fearless brushstrokes and heavily applied paint all came together to create the very foundations of modern art and a new way of "seeing" that had an enormous effect on future generations of artists. The unique painter who signed his work simply as "Vincent" influenced—and changed—the art world forever.

If you, or someone you know, is struggling with mental health or thinking about suicide, please call one of the twenty-four-hour crisis hotline numbers below right away.

1-800-662-HELP (4357)
Substance Abuse and Mental Health
Services Administration

988
Suicide & Crisis Lifeline

Timeline of Vincent van Gogh's Life

1853	Born March 30 in Groot-Zundert, Netherlands
1864	Starts at boarding school in Zevenbergen
1866	Moves to boarding school in Tilburg
1869	Works at The Hague gallery
1875	Moves to Paris, France
1878	Becomes an evangelical missionary in Borinage, Belgium
1880	Moves to Brussels to study art
1885	Paints *The Potato Eaters*, his first major painting
1886	Moves once again to Paris, France
1887	Paints *Self-Portrait with Straw Hat*
1888	Moves to Arles, France, in February
	Paints his most famous sunflower paintings; begins to suffer with mental health issues
	Cuts off portion of his ear (December)
1889	Commits himself to an asylum in Saint-Rémy, France (May)
	Paints *Irises* (May); paints *The Starry Night* (June)
1890	Paints *Almond Blossom* for his nephew (February)
	Leaves the asylum in Saint-Rémy and moves to Auvers under the care of Dr. Paul Gachet (May)
	Dies on July 29; buried at Auvers, France, on July 30

Timeline of the World

1853 — Solomon Northup, born a free Black man in New York, tells his story of being kidnapped and sold into slavery in the book *Twelve Years a Slave*

1860 — The Pony Express, an American mail service between Missouri and California, begins

1863 — US president Abraham Lincoln issues the Emancipation Proclamation

1864 — Elizabeth Jane Cochran, later known as Nellie Bly, pioneering female journalist and investigative reporter, is born on May 5

1865 — Lewis Carroll publishes *Alice's Adventures in Wonderland*

1867 — Alfred Nobel, whom the Nobel Prize is named after, invents dynamite

1872 — Yellowstone National Park, the first US national park, is created and signed into law by President Ulysses S. Grant

1879 — Thomas Edison tests his first light bulb

1885 — Louis Pasteur creates the first successful vaccine against rabies

1889 — The Eiffel Tower is inaugurated in Paris, France; Nellie Bly travels around the world in seventy-two days

1890 — The Wounded Knee massacre in South Dakota becomes the last battle in the American Indian Wars

Bibliography

*Books for young readers

Bailey, Martin. "Discovered: Van Gogh's Fingerprint on an Olive Grove Painting." *Art Newspaper*. March 25, 2022. https://www.theartnewspaper.com/2022/03/25/discovered-van-goghs-fingerprint-on-an-olive-grove-painting.

Boztas, Senay. "The Fingerprint and the Mystery Travels of a Van Gogh Painting." *Dutch News*. March 26, 2024. https://www.dutchnews.nl/2024/03/the-fingerprint-and-the-mystery-travels-of-a-van-gogh-painting/.

*Bucks, Brad, and Joan Holub. *Vincent van Gogh: Sunflowers and Swirly Stars*. New York: Grosset & Dunlap, 2001.

DK. *Great Paintings: The World's Masterpieces Explored and Explained*. New York: DK, 2011.

Gayford, Martin. *The Yellow House: Van Gogh, Gauguin, and the Nine Turbulent Weeks in Arles*. New York: Little Brown, 2006.

*Greenberg, Jan, and Sandra Jordan. ***Vincent van Gogh: Portrait of an Artist***. New York: Delacorte, 2001.

*Guglielmo, Amy. ***What the Artist Saw: Vincent van Gogh***. New York: DK, 2021.

Helvey, Jennifer. ***Irises: Vincent van Gogh in the Garden***. Los Angeles: J. Paul Getty Museum, 2009.

*Mühlberger, Richard. ***What Makes a Van Gogh a Van Gogh?*** New York: Viking, 1993.

Naifeh, Steven, and Gregory White Smith. ***Van Gogh: The Life***. New York: Random House, 2011.

Rapelli, Paola, and Alfredo Pallavisini. ***Van Gogh***. Masters of Art series. Munich: Prestel, 2016.

Saltzman, Cynthia. ***Portrait of Dr. Gachet: The Story of a Van Gogh Masterpiece, Money, Politics, Collectors, Greed, and Loss***. New York: Viking, 1998.